Published in the United States by
Maximum Change Press
Cincinnati, Ohio

www.maximumchange.com

Maximum Change is the registered trademark of Maximum Change, Inc. Open Organization is the registered trademark of Open Organization LLC, a wholly owned subsidiary of Maximum Change, Inc.

Cover Photo by Philip A Foster Copyright 2013.

ISBN-10: 061587844X

Table of Contents

Introduction

Leadership and organizational systems have been around since the beginning of civilization (Stone & Patterson, 2005, p.1). Beginning around 1500 through roughly 1000 B.C., the first known leadership hierarchies emerged as caste systems organized by hereditary distinctions based on occupation (In World History, 2013). Before caste systems, much of society was composed of nomadic tribes. The caste system created an evolution toward monarchy systems. Around 1000 to 967 BC, monarchs such as King David united the Israelite tribes and established a capital in Jerusalem (Girod, 2013). Leadership and organizational systems have greatly evolved over the past 5,000 years. As changes emerged, scholars began to adopt theoretical models to explain the processes and systems of leadership and organizational structures. These theoretical explanations progressed from caste systems and monarchies to *Great Man* theory and the classical approaches to leadership we engage today.

This book examines theories as they relate to three basic eras of leadership and organizational systems: Organization 1.0, Organization 2.0 and Organization 3.0.

A Brief History of Leadership

Leadership is defined as a process used by an individual to influence others toward a common goal (Penn, 2008, p. 1). The act of leadership presumes there are followers to lead and leaders, by their very nature, are expected to provide direction, exercise control, and generally execute such functions that are necessary to achieve the organization's objective (Kanungo & Mendonca, 1996, p. 2). The view of leadership and organizations has greatly evolved over time. Early organizations were led by authoritarian leaders who believed followers were intrinsically lazy (Stone & Patterson, p. 1). This belief has transitioned into ways in which we create work environments that are more conducive to increased productivity rates (Stone & Patterson, p. 1). However, the responsibility of a leader has evolved into reinforcing organizational goals through communication, participation and involvement and to break down old structures and establish new ones (Cummings &Worley, p. 158; Northouse, 2001, p. 144).

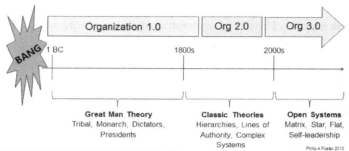

Figure 1:Timeline of Leadership & Organizational Theory.

Using the Timeline of Leadership and Organizational Theory (Figure 1), we see three distinct eras of time in which we can view the evolution of leadership and organizational theory. The first era, Organization 1.0 focuses predominantly on the *Great Man* theory and the emergence of Fredrick Taylor's *Scientific Management* approach to production. The *Scientific Management* approach naturally moves us into Organization 2.0, in which we find the emergence of *Classic Theories* of leadership and organizations. Finally, with increased complexity, globalism and emerging demographic trends we move swiftly into the newest era of Organization 3.0 in which leadership and organizations become flatter and decision making is driven by members of the organization through self-leadership and Autopoiesis methodologies. Within the structure of Organization 3.0, the traditional top-down hierarchy begins to be replaced with structures such as matrix, star, and open systems.

While there appears a beginning and end to each era, it is important to note that some scenarios, specifically organizations focused on command and control, will continue to focus on classical hierarchy systems found predominantly in Organization 2.0.

Organization 1.0 | 1 BC through early 1800s

The earliest studies of leadership theory focused on the characteristics and behaviors of successful leaders; while later theories consider the role of followers and the contextual nature of leadership (Bolden, et al, p. 6). In such case, the *Great Man* theory of Organization 1.0 essentially presumes that all great leaders are born.

The *Great Man* theory was developed in the early 1900s as leadership traits began to be studied to better determine what made certain people great leaders (Northouse, p. 15). The *Great Man* theory was predominately focused on identifying innate qualities and characteristics possessed by great social, political, and military leaders as it was thought that leaders possessed certain attributes that distinguished them from people who were not leaders (Northouse, p. 15). Up until this point in history, most all leaders were seen in the context of *Great Man* theory.

The *Great Man* theory fits well with a top-down hierarchy approach to leadership in that it assumes the leader at the top has a natural instinct for leadership and is placed in such a position out of some observable greatness. Top-down leadership follows the *Great Man* theory in that a top-down organization is a traditional model whose concept is borrowed from centuries of war, military hierarchy, dictatorships and monarchies. The focus of such an organization is on the leader at the top of the chain of command. For example, the CEO is in command and there are many layers between them and the customer. We can see from this traditional model that the front lines in this model are the employees. In a top-down organization, everyone focuses on the boss and away from the customer (Homula, 2010).

Toward the end of the Organization 1.0 era, early in the 20th century, management emerged as a field of study introduced by Frederick W. Taylor (Gordon, 1991, p. 16). It is during this era the United States saw mass immigration and the workplace was being flooded with unskilled, uneducated workers (Walton, 1986, p. 8). Taylor, a foreman at the Bethlehem Steel Works in Bethlehem, Pennsylvania introduced the *Scientific Method* (Gordon, p. 16) which was believed to be an efficient way to employ larger numbers of labor as well as reduce conflict and eliminate arbitrary uses of power by leaders (Walton, p. 9). Taylor and others began to believe that management could be studied and applied through scientific process (Walton, p. 9). Taylor's structure and design of management activities stated managers and employees held clearly specified yet different responsibilities (Gordon, p. 16). Taylor's approach required managers to develop precise, standard procedures for doing each job, select workers with appropriate abilities, train workers in the standard procedures, carefully plan out all their work and provide wage incentives to increase employee output (Daft, 2004, p. 25). Hence, the rule-bound, top-heavy American corporate structure was born (Walton, p. 9). While Taylor's system did produce larger quantities, it was cumbersome and rigid and therefore was slow to adjust to market conditions (Walton, p. 9). The process created the assumption that the role of management was to maintain stability and efficiency, with top managers doing the thinking and workers doing what they are told to do (Daft, p. 25).

Taylor's approach to leadership and organizational structure naturally gave rise to other theorists and the emergence of classic leadership and organizational theories found in the era of Organization 2.0.

Organization 2.0 | Early 1800s through late 1990s

Entering the era of Organization 2.0, we find several schools of thought or perspectives related to leadership and organizational theories. Toward the end of the Organization 1.0 era, Taylor's theories created an interest in understanding the way leadership and organizations should behave. With this growing emphasis we began to witness a growing emphasis on a structural perspective to theory in which we call Organization 2.0. This era can best be described as the era of *Classical Leadership* and *Organizational* theory development, which spanned most of the 20th century.

Included in this school of thought we find the *Classical School* in which employees have specific but different responsibilities; are scientifically selected, trained and development of workers and division of work between those workers and management is equal (Gordon, p. 15). In addition, the *Bureaucracy* school of thinking emphasized order, systems, rationality, uniformity, and consistency in management; these attributes led to equitable treatment for all employees by management (Gordon, p. 15).

By the 1920s however, structural perspectives of administration gave way to behavioral perspectives of leadership and organizational thought. Beginning with *Human Relations*, organizations began to focus on the importance of the attitudes and feelings of workers and it was determined informal roles and norms influenced performance (Gordon, p. 15). The *Classical School* briefly reappeared as a reemphasis on the classical principles of chain-of-command and coordination of activities previously developed in the 1910s (Gordon, p. 15). By the 1940s *Group Dynamics* began to encourage individuals to participate in decision making and by the 1950s the *Leadership School* stressed the importance of groups having both social and task leaders (Gordon, p. 15).

Decision Theory (Behavioral perspective), *Sociotechnical School, Systems Theory and Environmental and Technological Analysis Theories* (Integrative perspective) emerged in the 1960s. *Decision Theory* suggested that individuals "satisfice" when they make decisions (Gordon, p. 15). *Sociotechnical School* called for the consideration of technology and work groups when understanding the work system in which we operate (Gordon, p. 15). *Systems Theory* offered the first glimpse of an emerging Organization 3.0 era as it represented an organization as an *Open System* with inputs, transformations, outputs, and feedback where systems strive for equilibrium and experience equifinality (Gordon, p. 15). Next, *Environmental and Technological Analysis Theories* described the existence of mechanistic and organic structures and stated their effectiveness with specific types of environmental conditions and technological types (Gordon, p. 15). Finally, in the 1980s, the emergence of the last integrative perspective known as *Contingency Theory* emphasized the fit between organizational processes and characteristics of a given situation (Gordon, p.15).

The distinction between Organization 1.0 and Organization 2.0 was a movement away from the emphasis of the manager and placed it on the employees. However, influence still played a role in how managers were able to lead others. In modern application leaders are to be competent in that they hold knowledge of a given topic, intelligence, expertise, skill or good judgment (Hackman & Johnson, 2000, p. 163). When competence is found, a leader can then influence a group of individuals to achieve a common goal (Northouse, p. 3). In fact, in the era of Organization 2.0, leadership occurred in groups and involved influencing groups of individuals (Northouse, p. 3). The *Classical Theories* of Organization 2.0 forward the thought that for an organization to thrive, leaders and employees need to understand how structure and context (organizational theory) are related to interactions among diverse employees (organizational behavior) to accomplish to the goals and objectives of the organization (Daft, p. 34).

In the Organization 2.0 era, leadership might be defined in terms of the power relationship that exists between leaders and followers (Northouse, p. 2). Leaders exert their power and influence on the environment through three types of actions: 1) goals and performances standards they establish, 2) the values they establish for the organization and 3) the business and people concepts they establish (Clark, 2004). Successful organization begin to see leaders who set high standards and goals across the entire spectrum, such as strategies, market leadership, plans, meetings and presentations, productivity and reliability (Clark). Organization values began to reflect concern for employees, customers, investors, vendors, and surrounding community (Clark).

Historically we find many theories, including *Great Man* and *Top-Down*, which deal with leadership and its influences over subordinates in varying degrees. During the Organization 2.0 era, leaders began to seek the "secret formula" of leadership theory in their pursuit of effective organizational transformation. One viable option considered was the *Leader-Follower* theory. A *Leader-Follower* implies a system of two or more persons working together at any one time, where leaders assume followers' roles and followers assume leadership roles (Pitron, 2008; Gilbert & Matviuk, 2008). Unlike traditional definitions of leadership, this approach claims followership and leadership are not so much about position, but about their ability to influence through behaviors and self-concept (Gilbert & Matviuk). Followers and leaders both orbit around the purpose; followers do not orbit around the leader (Chaleff, 2003). The concept of *Leader-Follower* contrasts with traditional approaches to leadership such as *Great Man* and *Top-Down* theories. The *Leader-Follower* theory pushes followers beyond the context of subordinate and obedience and opens the opportunity for innovation and change within an organization otherwise

unrealized in the *Great Man* and *Top-Down* organizational

models. Evidence shows those organizations where the

Leader-Follower methodology is in use yield individuals who

desire investment in their jobs and the organization as a

whole.

Beyond theory and structure, Organization 2.0

introduced the need for critical thinking, which examined

assumption, discerned hidden values, evaluated evidence, and

assessed conclusions (Meyers, 2007, p. 24). Critical thinking

requires distinguishing between strategic planning and

strategic thinking. Strategic thinking requires thinking

through the plan to determine likely unintended

consequences. Much of the traditional strategic planning

models were heavily oriented to quantitative analysis

(Mendenhall, 2011). While quantitative processes are not in

question, these planning models actually subverted strategic thinking that involve the synthesis of one's experience, intuition, and creativity, in addition to analysis (Mendenhall).

During the Organization 2.0 era, values and ethics also grew in importance. Values and ethics or trust is based on an employee's perception of the leader's reliability and dependability as a result of past follow-through on their commitments (Davis & Rothstein, 2006, p. 408). Trust and credibility is tied to psychological contracting which is a perceived (either verbal or implied) agreement between two parties and is born from a belief that a promise of some future return has been made and that an obligation to future benefits has been created (Davis & Rothstein, pp. 408-9). Leaders became part of the *soul of the organization* as they set the tone as to how things were to be done around the organization (Foster, 2011). For example, if a leader is consistently late, it is difficult for them to effectively require their followers to adhere to company attendance policies. Behavioral integrity is therefore perceived to be low because of a mismatch between expressed values and the values expressed through actions (Simons, 1999, p. 90). It was found that leaders developed trust by their consistency in moral judgments, values and character. Character is something that must manifest not only in the leaders public life but throughout their entire life (HRMID, 2011, p. 6).

Values formation within an organization is an approach to life that impacts all members within the organization (Grace, 2011). Moreover there appears to be a correlation between effective leadership and how much autonomy is given to the followers. A leader who does not trust their followers appear to have the most trouble with change. Such a resistance to change appears linked to a shared commitment of beliefs which encourages consistency in an organization's behaviors, and thereby discourages change in strategy (Mintzberg, et al., 1998, p. 269). When change fails to occur within the organization as planned, the cause is always to be found at a deeper level, rooted in the inappropriate behavior, beliefs, attitudes, and assumptions of would-be leaders (O'Toole, 1996, p. x). Organizations can benefit greatly from a leader who understands the influence they hold on the values of their organization. Unfortunately most organizations are led by leaders who only know how to be administrators (Hamel, 2002, p. 22). Leaders who do not understand the role they serve create a misalignment and instill inappropriate values in those they lead. An effective leader would almost always begin with a commitment to the moral principles of respect for the followers (O'Toole, p. 34). Ultimately, followers create a perceived notion of the leader's character. Character is what makes a leader worth following (Stanley, 2003, p. 131).

Before the 1960s, traditional theories only looked at organizations as closed, isolated systems however, over time theorists added humanistic and holistic ideologies to the mix (Griffin, n.d.). Predominantly, these traditional theories ignored outside environmental influences such as natural disasters, social changes, political changes and even employees' personal problems (Griffin, n.d.). With that, Organization 2.0 began to produce a greater emphasis on organizational structures, systems and environments and our understanding of organizational structures, boundaries and communication from within and sometimes outside the confines of the organization. What began to emerge was a sense that organizations must be flexible and adaptable enough to enable managers to forward plan in context of constantly changing operating environments (Stanford, 2009, p. 69). Toward the end of the 20th century as the economy attempted to recover and organizations maintained relatively smaller staff; organizations began facing globalization, advances in technology, diverse workforce, greater segmentation in the customer base, attuned investors and competition both traditional global players and smaller innovators (Hesselbein & Goldsmith, 2009, p. 15).

Organizational capabilities emerged as the last true sustainable source of competitive advantage (Nadler & Tushman, 1997, p. 226). Organizational design required an assessment of the current structure and its ability to deliver future results and which are in alignment with other organizational attributes (Stanford, p. 46). Such designs must direct sufficient attention to the sources of the organizations competitive advantage in each market in which it serves (Stanford, p 46). Organizational design was not limited to structure as leaders were also considered as part of the design that keeps the structure in alignment (Branch, 2011). In context of organizational design, leaders must: balance the demands of daily activities with the demands of specific projects; manage competing priorities, tasks and activities; assist followers to cope with inevitable change; satisfy business needs quickly while getting it done right; get the timing right on leadership issues; motivate all stakeholders whose input is critical to the project; and ability to work effectively with other leaders within and without the project and/or organization (Stanford, p 189). As we neared the end of the 20th century, non-traditional organizations began to break free of their former rigidity and developed different shapes, working habits, age profiles and differing traditions of authority (Handy, 1989, p. 15).

Pressures on organizational design increased and the view of centralized systems began to shift. While a centralized system has a clear leader who is in charge and there is a specific location where decisions are made, a decentralized system has no clear leader, structure or central location (Brafman & Beckstrom, 2006, p. 19). The benefit of a decentralized system was its agility under pressure. When a decentralized system is attacked it becomes more decentralized and more difficult to stop (Brafman & Beckstrom, p. 21). The decentralized system is not necessarily a better organization or better at making decisions in-so-much as it is able to more quickly respond to changing conditions because all members of the system have access to knowledge and hold the ability to make decisions (Brafman & Beckstrom, p. 39). The true role of organizational design is to develop adaptability, flexibility and profitability in the most efficient and effective manger available, given the resources available to it. Organizations of the future will continue to adapt and develop a spirit of learning and growth. The organization of the future will need to focus on creativity, innovations as it develops and modifies to meet the constant changing needs of the world in which it serves.

Leaving the 20th century we find a time of unprecedented globalization of organizations and economies. Understanding the effects of culture had a large impact on an organizations ability to achieve success. Organizational decision-making styles began to be influenced by generational and cultural attributes of the individuals from within the organizational system. The advent of the Internet and other technologies began to link individuals across cultures;

creating collaborations unheard of in centuries past. Through this reality, leaders began to understand the impact a globalized economy brings to the doors of their organizations. Accessibility of information and goods via the Internet opens doors for nearly every business to compete globally. In fact, if an organization has an Internet presence, they are, by its very definition a global organization. As the global economy arrives and leaders step forward into the global arena, they must understand geography, language, customs, values, ethics, varying laws and national psychologies will all determine their success within the global marketplace. Leaders and their organizations must learn to move beyond their own worldview and open themselves to the complexities of cultures, geography, laws, customers and languages that await them. Leaders who take the time to become culturally literate will best develop relationships that positively impact their organization. Developing relationships is essential to the success of any leader who seeks to operate in the global context. Developing relationships builds respect, trust, and creates understanding. Developing relationships of trust creates freedom amongst the followers to self-initiate solutions to problems without delay or confusion. These cultural nuances become essential to the overall success of the leader from within the culture they operate.

Organization 3.0 | 1990s through the 2000s

While the Organization 1.0 era was focused entirely on the leader and Organization 2.0 focused on the *Classical Theories*, the era of Organization 3.0 began to focus on organizational design and its effects on employee behavior. In this new era, we no longer rely on the traditional models of design structure, function and employee interaction. The business climate of the early 21st century almost instinctively requires organizations and its members to become more agile in their response to ever changing economic conditions. Organizations must now learn to develop processes to share knowledge and resources across boundaries to achieve stated goals. Organizational design requires new approaches and innovative ways of thinking. The world is pressed on all sides by a diminishing full-time workforce as well as differing cultural, generational, political, and religious views. The organization of the 21st century must be more agile than its 19th and 20th century ancestors. Organizational design is essential to how the organization deals with the challenges it now faces.

In the early part of the 21st century, organizations engaged in a frenzy of structural realignments that led to acquisitions, divestitures, joint ventures, outsourcing, and alliances (Ashkenas, et al., 2002, p. xxvii). The era of Organization 3.0 has witnessed change at a historically unprecedented rate. In this new era, organizations must find ways to adapt to the changing world. In 1989 it was predicted that by the year 2000, less than half of the workforce in the industrialized world would be in "proper" full-time jobs and that before long full-time employees would be the minority (Handy, pp. 31, 34). The organization of the future must structure itself around new realities of globalization, technology, diverse employees, and customer demands (Hesselbein & Goldsmith, p. 15). More than ever, organizations must find organic approaches to dealing with change and innovation. One such emerging concept is that of

a decentralized matrix style organization, otherwise defined
as an *Open Organization*. The end result of an *Open
Organization* is not to abolish organizational structure but to
create a more flexible flow of ideas and processes that meets
the needs of each individual within the organization as they
pursue the goals of the organization and its stakeholders.

The *Open Organization* begins to recognize that
individuals, groups, and organizations have needs that must
be satisfied. It is this kind of thinking that now underpins the
idea of an *Open Organizational* approach, which takes its
main inspiration from the work of Ludwig von Bartalanffy, a
theoretical biologist (Morgan, 2006, p. 38). Developed in the
1950s and 1960s, the systems approach builds on the
principle that organizations, like organisms, are "open" to
their environment and must achieve an appropriate relation
with that environment if they are to survive (Morgan, p. 38).

The *Open Organization* concept is gaining attention
as it enables teams to develop products and services within

diverse production models, communication methodologies and interactive communities (Elmquist, et al., 2009, p. 329; Open Organization, 2006). An *Open Organization* is defined as the sharing of ideas, knowledge, resources, and skills across organizational, generational and cultural boundaries within, and in some cases outside, an organizational system for the purpose of achieving a stated outcome (Foster). The *Open Organization* model permits teams to carry out several projects at once through the use of differing approaches and agendas in an effort to expel the use of centralized models and hierarchical teams (Open Organization). The main attribute of an *Open Organization* is in the peer interaction which crosses organizational, generational and cultural boundaries to collaborate with others for the expressed purpose of producing an end-product and sharing the source-materials, blueprints, and documentation freely within the organization (Open Organization). There are four key factors to implementing an *Open* system: 1) broaden the organizations view, 2) create alignment across organization ecosystems, 3) adapt an approach for organizational risk tolerance, and 4) focus the organization on learning rather than just results (Docherty, 2006, p 64).

An *Open Organization* is simply a method of self-leadership in which individuals participate in the movement of an organization from their strengths (Foster, p. 2). An *Open Organization* is a decentralized structure which trends away from authoritarian management styles, separatist titles and privileges of multilevel hierarchies found mostly in Organization 1.0 and 2.0 (Galbraith, 2002, p. 17). Nontraditional organizations such as an *Open Organization* lead to faster decision making, lower overhead and leaders who are more in touch with their followers (Galbraith, p. 20). Non-traditional organizations, such as an *Open Organization,* are considered more flexible which will require individuals who are generalists and can cooperate openly with one another (Galbraith, p. 13). Unlike the centralized system of the Organization 1.0 and 2.0 eras, an *Open Organization* may, at times, appear to not have a clear leader who is in charge or a specific location where decisions are made (Brafman & Beckstom, p. 19). The benefit of a decentralized system is found in its agility under pressure. It is not necessarily a better organization or better at making decisions in-so-much as it is able to more quickly respond to changing conditions because all members of the system have access to knowledge and hold the ability to make decisions (Brafman & Beckstrom, p. 39).

While there is no one-size-fits-all approach to organizational design, an organization behaves in the ways it has been designed to behave (Stanford, p. 3). An *Open Organization* requires that everyone in the organization have some control over what is going on and it requires all members have an equal voice in the process (Stanford, p. 28). You would therefore expect to find a strong level of accountability by all members within an *Open Organization*

(Foster, 2011, p. 12). The process of being accountable would make it necessary for all members to intervene in the decision-making process when another member does not meet their obligations (Foster, p. 12). An *Open Organizational* system requires all members to let go of their preconceived notions of how people operate and essentially trust in faith that the people to whom you pass the power to will act responsibly (Li, 2010, p. 18). The biggest indicator of success of an *Open Organizational* system comes from an open-mind and the leader's ability to give control over to the followers at the right time and place and to the extent which people need the discretion to get their job done (Li, p. 8).

Within the Organization 3.0 era, traditional hierarchical structures are becoming flatter as the emphasis of structural design is placed on specialization, shape, distribution of power, and departmentalization and its impact on the leaders, followers and clients (Galbraith, p. 17-18). In this era, decentralized organizations have a better chance of

surviving and more effectively adapting to the culture, current
business climate, increasing competitiveness and attacks in
general because it is autonomous and is more agile in its
ability to react to changing conditions (Brafman & Beckstrom,
p. 48-49).

An *Open Organization* in no way signifies that it is
void of formal structure or leadership. In fact, an *Open
Organization* very much relies on a framework on which to
build and the leadership element very much remains a central
requirement of an open system (Yehuda, 2001). While
organizations may vary in how open they are to their
environments, even an *Open Organization* will display a
hierarchical ordering in which each of its higher level of
systems comprise of lower-level systems such as: systems at
the level of society comprise of organizations; organizations
comprise of groups or departments; and groups comprise of
individuals (Cummings & Worley, p. 85). An *Open
Organization* will not only maintain a structure but also

utilizes a set of standards called an organizational governance or charter. An *Open Organizations* charter explicitly lays out how members within the system will work together without having to negotiate individual agreements with each member (Li, p. 34). The structure which emerges must exist independent of any organizational compensation or rewards systems that seek to reward individuals disproportionately and most often associated with a formal business model (O'Mahony, 2007). To accomplish this framework requires the organization to develop a formal written charter that ensures that the interest of all members is represented and provides independent decision-making at all levels of the organization free from any single external controlling influence (O'Mahony). A formal governance or charter provides operational standards which aim to facilitate the dissemination of information and content throughout the *Open Organizational* system (Open Archive, 2011). While *Open Organizations* are not leaderless; they are very much lead in such a way that leverages new behaviors within the system (Yehuda). In fact, it could be argued that an *Open Organization* is an organization of leaders. Beyond self-leadership, leaders are still required to manage, measure, correct, take control and hold accountability for given results (Yehuda). Depending on the level of openness within the organization will determine to what extent the leadership will operate. An *Open Organization* is much like the leader-follower theory in that the leader in no way abdicates the role of leadership within the organization.

The structure of most traditional business models of the Organization 2.0 era are typically recognized as having a closed decision-making (Open Organizations). Individuals within the organizations are un-accountable, knowledge is hoarded and there is likely to be some kind of abuse of power (Open Organizations). Counter to the traditional organizational mode, *Open Organizations* typically rely on trust and the free flow of ideas and information amongst the members within the confines of the organizational structure and governance. The free flow of ideas encourages the ability for members to creatively solve problems that will arise in the course of a business cycle (Simoes-Brown, 2009, p. 51). Creativity may even result in the development of ideas and information between the organization and its clients. Such creativity requires all members of the system to suspend judgment and allow for new ideas and opinions to be expressed (Simoes-Brown, p. 51). The result of a free, unencumbered sharing of ideas, allows for unconventional and innovative approaches to develop and grow (Simoes-Brown, p. 51).

It is generally accepted that organizations have some kind of formal lines of communication and dissemination of work assignments is directed and does not necessarily account for individual motivational needs. When organizations do consider motivational needs of the followers, there remain rigid organizational mandates before any of the needs of the individuals will be considered. The best scenario for success would be an organizational model that champions the intrinsic motivational needs of the individual while facilitating the expressed needs of the organization. Creating a flexible environment that meets the needs of both the organization and its members is a challenge for leaders. A more organic organizational approach would certainly satisfy both. For example, a vine has structure but is flexible and can make changes as challenges arise. Such flexibility affords the vine the ability to navigate around obstacles, yet maintain the structure required to move nutrients throughout the entire system of vine. The challenge is to translate the vine analogy into an organizational mechanism that permits the structure to reach specified goals.

In considering an organic approach to sourcing information, the open system offers a solution to meet organizational needs. The *Open Organization* model includes the concept of concurrent yet different agendas and differing approaches in production, which is in contrast with more centralized models of development such as those typically used in hierarchical teams. A main principal and practice of *Open Organization* teams is the peer interaction across team and organizational boundaries through collaboration with the resulting product, source-materials, blueprints, and documentation made freely available to all members of the organization (Open Organization). Open systems create organizational structures that are less rigid than its more formal structured hierarchical counterparts. The end result is not to abolish organizational structure but to create a more flexible flow of ideas and processes that meets the motivational needs of each individual within the organization as they pursue the goals of the organization. Within an *Open Organization*, the decision-making process must be highly inclusive and it must allow consensus to emerge where it exists (Ousterhout, 2009).

The idea of an open system reveals a fundamental truth that the best person to a do a given job is typically the one who most wants to do that job and the best people to evaluate the individuals performance are those who will enthusiastically pitch in to help improve the final product out of the sheer pleasure of helping one another achieve something from which they all will receive benefit (Howe, 2008, p. 8). The nature of an *Open Organization* has revealed that, contrary to conventional wisdom, individuals do not always behave in so-called predictable self-interested patterns (Howe, p. 15). Individuals will typically participate for little or no money, laboring tirelessly despite financial reward through the mechanics of collective intelligence, a large number of people are able to contribute and aggregate information and solutions to come up with better solutions (Howe, pp. 15, 54, 180). An *Open Organization* does not mean that the members are able to make better decisions, but that they are able to respond more quickly because they have access to a collective

knowledge and the ability to make use of it (Brafman &
Beckstrom, pp. 39-40).

In the era of Organization 3.0 we find organizations
increasingly comprised of individuals from differing cultural
origins. Therefore, understanding the effects culture has on
an organization is important to the success of it becoming
more open. Not only can culture act as a prism that blinds
organizational leaders to changing external conditions, but
even when those leaders overcome their cultural myopia, they
respond to changing events in terms of their own cultural lens
and they tend to stick with the beliefs that have worked for
them in the past (Mintzberg, et al., p. 270). Culture remains
complex because it is essentially composed of individual
interpretations of the world and the activities and artifacts
that reflect these interpretations (Mintzberg, et al., p. 265).
An organization must contain collective beliefs for the
argument of all cultural elements to be self-evident
(Mintzberg, et al., p. 265). Resistance to change appears

linked to a shared commitment to beliefs which encourages consistency in an organization's behaviors, and thereby discourages any changes in strategy (Mintzberg, et al., p. 269). Culture acts as a perceptual filter or lens in which individuals establish the premise for their decisions (Mintzberg, et al., p. 269). Arguably, it boils down to how a person's worldview may influence organizational thinking.

Organization 3.0 operates in a globalized market. Globalization forces us to consider worldviews and cultural difference which are determined by the psychic distance or cultural distance between the home or existing geography and the new geography (Galbraith, p 49). Cultural difference is greater for countries with different language, religions, political systems, economic systems, legal systems, levels of development, and education (Galbraith, p. 49). Simply put, it is easier for organizations to operate within countries that have the smallest cultural distance and the lowest learning curve (Galbraith, p. 49). Sire (1997) prompts us to consider our own worldview or presuppositions which we hold about the basic makeup of the world around us (p. 16). Considering our own worldview helps us to understand the challenges multinational companies have in their integration of activities that take place in different countries (Galbraith, p. 3). There are societal/cultural risks associated with operating within differing sociocultural environments (de Kluyver & Pearce, p. 200). Considering your own worldview or cultural influence therefore is an essential element of an *Open Organizations* success. When autonomy and self-management are important aspects of the organizations, then matters of culture are less of an issue.

Barriers to success exist in nearly any business environment. Operating an *Open Organization* within a global context adds new layers and challenges related to languages, customs, values, traditions and laws. Challenging these barriers will certainly create friction and can affect our ability to listen and understand the viewpoints on those we lead. Lack of understanding creates frustration, mistakes and deters trust and relationship building between the leader and their followers. Learning local customs and language is helpful; however there is no easy fix to these barriers. Creating greater understanding through language is the mechanism that helps people organize their perceptions and shape their worldviews (Hackman & Johnson, p. 297). A global leader's ability to connect people and build successful teams in a cross-cultural environment is a crucial competency with the Organization 3.0 era (Johnson, 2012). In dealing with cross-cultural communication we must acknowledge that communication encompasses not only words and actions, but also all types of non-verbal communication and patterns of interaction in society at large (Eisenberg & Goodall, 2004, p. 139). Building a cross-cultural relationships require an ability to process or decode information from our environment as well as learning to effectively encode by conveying messages and then taking the most appropriate actions to overcome problems (Northouse, p. 165). The ideal scenario for any cross-cultural organization would be the creation of synergy by which decision-makers draw on the diversity of the group to produce a new, better than expected solution (Hackman & Johnson, p 305).

In considering cross-cultural patterns within an organization, power distance is an important attribute to consider in the development of a cross-cultural communication strategy within an *Open Organization*. Power distance is the extent to which the less powerful members of institutions and organizations within a culture expect and accept that power is distributed unequally (Tamas, 2007). All societies are unequal and within high power-distance cultures, the inequality is considered to be a natural part of their world while in contrast, low power-distance cultures are uncomfortable with differences in wealth, status, power and privilege (Hackman & Johnson, p. 302). Power distance, specifically high-power distance cultures, can become a barrier to the successful operation of an *Open Organization* as they do not accept the equal distribution of power. An *Open Organization* requires little power distance between leaders and followers. The greater the distance between a leader and their followers, the closer the supervision of the follower's activities and the less open an organization becomes (Hackman & Johnson, p. 302). Followers in high power-distance countries expect managers to give direction and feel uncomfortable when asked to participate in decision making (Hackman & Johnson, p 302). This creates a challenge in an *Open Organization* where followers are expected to make their own decisions with little input from leadership. Organizations operating in low power-distance countries are less centralized and distribute rewards more equally (Hackman & Johnson, p 302). Low power-distance cultures, by nature, have an easier time developing and operating within the context of an open system.

Beyond Organization 3.0

Organization 3.0 offers a view of what the future holds for leaders and organizations. While knowing what will happen in the future is not possible; we can anticipate possible future conditions so that we can better prepare for them (McGuffey, 2012; Cornish, 2004, p. 65). One area of deficit for most leaders is the ability to anticipate future possibilities and weigh them against opportunities and risks their organizations may face (Cornish, p. 65). This creates a challenge for those organizations attempting to compete in the new global landscape. The era beyond Organization 3.0 will require leaders who develop long-range planning skills and are able to navigate changes in very short windows of time. The more we expect the unexpected by considering the possibilities of the unexpected, the greater opportunity we find for success (Cornish, p. 4). Preparing for the unexpected can be achieved by many methods; whether by simulations and games or by lists, processes or techniques, considering future possibilities helps us better prepare mentally and otherwise for the eventualities a possible future may hold.

Scenario analysis has emerged as one of the most widely used techniques for constructing plausible futures of an organizations external environment (de Kluyver & Pearce, p. 70). Scenario planning is certainly a skill our future leaders must acquire if they are to compete in 21st century. For many, the concept of scenario analysis ends with strategic planning which was originally billed as a way of becoming more future oriented even though most managers admit that their strategic plans reveal more about today's problems than the opportunities of tomorrow (Senge, 1990, p. 210). In fact, creative strategies seldom come from annual planning rituals of the three to five year plan as the company will likely stick to market segments it knows, even though there may be opportunities elsewhere (Senge, p. 214). Because most strategic plans of the past were developed with the three to five year mindset, they were most often focused only on what they already knew about the organizations performance and current direction rather than what could be.

Without scenarios, companies may become blindsided by future possibilities (Schoemaker, 2002, p. 46). An example of missing future possibilities is that of Encyclopedia Britannica. Britannica began in the book business but evolved, nearly overnight, into an information business (Schoemaker, p. 46). In 1989, Britannica was at the top of the industry but by 1994 sales slipped 53 percent as other companies offered more exciting electronic alternatives at a lessor cost and great ease of consumer use (Schoemaker, p. 46). Unfortunately Britannica failed to anticipate the future of its industry and by 1996 its sales dropped by 70 percent (Schoemaker, p. 46). Considering potential scenarios can help organizations such as Britannica avoid tunnel vision and overconfidence which ultimately could be their ruin (Schoemaker, p. 46). Britannica was caught in the norm of focusing on the known and either was unable to or unwilling to step outside of its comfort zone to attack the unknowns, even with opportunities awaiting them (Schoemaker, p. 47). Using scenarios planning and analysis, Britannica, could have identified different possible drivers of change and begin to consider future alternatives through the process of scenario analysis.

One of the problems we face in the 21st century is that most business literature has focused mainly on organizational strategy and vision rather than the concept of flexible long-range strategic planning known as strategic foresight. Therefore, many of today's leaders have been trained with this narrow mindset. Rather than the short-range goal setting process taught in most traditional business schools, strategic foresight is the use of techniques and frameworks of hypothetically standing in the future to understand where the organization may be (Marsh, et al., 2002, p. 2). Strategic foresight is about creating new perspectives on key issues concerning an organization today through an integrated

approach to strategy which results in discovery and
articulation of a preferred direction for the organization
(Marsh, et al., p. 2 – 4). Strategic foresight follows
hypothetical cases which describe an organizations response
to crisis management, opportunity management, risk
management and potential changes in a given sector (Marsh,
et al., p. 11). Leaders may best incorporate foresight
methodologies through the framework focused on what would
be most critical to an organizations success (Hines, 2006, p.
18). For leaders to determine the strategic direction of their
organization, they must look inward, outward, and forward
while scanning both the internal and external organizational
environments to identify trends, threats and opportunities for
the organization (Daft, 2002, p. 495). Strategic foresight is a
skill which enables leaders to anticipate the risks and
opportunities they may confront in the future (Cornish, p. xi).
Foresight permits us to mentally stand in the future and
imagine what it might be like and then return to the present

day with possible insights to help us understand our potential future (Marsh, et al., p. 2). Foresight allows managers to discover and articulate a preferred diction for their organization and then focus on what would be most critical to an organization's success in the future (Marsh, et al., p. 4; Hines, p. 18).

Foresight is the imagined possibilities and innovation is the expected solution to those possibilities. Therefore, foresight is *what* can be expected and innovation is *how* we react to future possibilities. The goal of forecasting is not to predict the future but to tell you what you need to know to take meaningful action in the present (Saffo, 2012, p. 72). Once we stand in the future and look back to the present, issues concerning us now begin to look differently rather than unimportant (Marsh, et al., p. 2). The concept of *standing in the future* allows us to create an *unrestricted view* of the future as we are now free to realize that the future is not predetermined and thus something we necessarily need to react to or cope with (Marsh, et al., p. 2). Strategic foresight is a way of thinking, engaging, discovering, and acting as a way to discovering crucial factors and sharing in the exploration of trends and change related to the future and relies on a framework focused on what would be most critical to an organization (Marsh, et al., p. 5; Hines, p. 18). Through the act of forecasting we realize the fluidity of potentials and the imagination of possibilities enhances our ability to act reasonably to the issues before us.

To best prepare for the eras beyond Organization 3.0 we must consider taxonomies or paradigms in mapping out the terrain of the futures through: scanning, trend analysis, trend monitoring, trend projection, scenarios, polling, brainstorming, modeling, gaming, historical analysis, and visioning. These taxonomies rely on modeling to represent or simulate actions and their results (Gary, 2012; Cornish, p. 70, 78-79). Taxonomies are used to anticipate, forecast, or assess future events (Cornish, p. 78). Considering scenario planning, we look toward trends, strategies, and wildcard events to create awareness of potential future events that may or may not validate the desired course of actions for the organization (Cornish, p. 79). In essence, scenarios help us navigate toward our preferred future outcome. The use of systems and taxonomies create proper decision funnels for practitioners of foresight. Finding ways to assimilate these changes without threat becomes important to organizational growth and change.

Current trends appear to indicate that the future of organizations is best seen through a lens of alliances and collaboration. Perhaps the most compelling trend driving this shift; less than half of the work force in the industrial world is in "proper" full-time employment by the beginning of the 21st century (Handy, p. 31). In fact, in a 2011 Gallup poll, 40 percent of the industrialized world was in full time positions. As the landscape of employment and human capital changes, organizations must consider structures that account for decreasing numbers of full-time employees and increasing numbers of part-time, temporary and consultant/contract labor (Foster, p. 4). The 21st century organizational design will require an ability to share ideas, knowledge, resources and skills across organizational, generational and cultural boundaries within and outside of the organizational system for the purpose of achieving desired goals (Foster). As organizations become more open and employment trends continue their downward push of less full-time employment, it is anticipated organizations will need to adopt new models to engage human capital.

To meet shifting demands, organizations of the future may be composed of one of three types of alliance structures: the *operator model* in which one partner takes on the management responsibility of the joint activity; the *shared model* in which the responsibilities are divided equally amongst the members; or the *joint venture* in which the activities can be autonomous (Galbraith, p 149). Alliances illuminate gaps in the strategy that would have otherwise been unaddressed without this particular alliance/joint venture in place. The formation of an alliance creates influence without having or using formal authority (Gordon, p. 417). This influence will become necessary for employees who are seeking to compete in a complex, globalized marketplace. Alliances form when individuals have resources or favors to exchange and they can occur between peers, supervisors and subordinates, or among members of different organizations, they are also the culmination of a larger pool of resources to a given situation, including greater expertise and commitment (Gordon, p. 418). Regardless of what goals or objectives an alliance is meant to achieve, there must be buy-in or sponsorship from upper level leaders and executives. Emerging factors favoring the formation of alliance groups is the growing complexity of products and services and of their design, production and delivery (Gomes-Casseres, 1994). While some alliances are meant to be long term, some alliances are no more than fleeting encounters, lasting only as long as it takes one partner to establish a beachhead in a new market or perhaps even the prelude to a full merger of two or more company's technologies and capabilities (Kanter, 1994).

Conclusion

The 21st century organization will require an ability to share ideas, knowledge, resources and skills across organizational, generational and cultural boundaries within and outside of the organizational system for the purpose of achieving desired goals. The world will continue to become smaller as technology advances and organizations grow in diversity of individuals from differing cultures and geographical locales. Organizational decision-making styles will grow in influence by generational and cultural attributes of the individuals from within the organizational system.

The challenge for organizations is to find a design that will address generational, cultural, industry, geographical and other environmental factors in which it must compete. Organizations that do not anticipate the need to adapt to changing circumstances will likely underperform and ultimately go out of business (Stanford, p. 1). What we strive for is an appropriate structure that aligns organizational mission/vision, values, principles, strategies, objectives, tactics, systems, structures, people, processes, cultures and performance measures in such a way as to deliver consistent effective results (Stanford, p. 8). The best scenario for success would be an organizational model that would integrate the intrinsic motivational needs of the individual while facilitating the expressed needs of the organization. Creating a flexible environment that meets the needs of both is a challenge for the leaders of the future. The organization of the 21st century must focus on creativity and innovations as it develops and modifies itself to meet the constant changing needs of the world in which it serves. While the use of open systems is not yet a widely used organizational model; the *Open Organization* offers competitive market flexibility while meeting intrinsic motivational needs of its members in a structured work environment that is collaborative, autonomous, transparent, generationally inclusive, and cultural diverse.

As organizations become more globally integrated and move toward flatter more open structures, leading from a global context becomes a complex matter rooted in an ability to understand and connect with a given culture and its people. Given that *Open Organizations* rely heavily on an ability to share information across all boundaries, they must develop ways to connect with individuals within a given culture and improve the quality of their decisions through the development of close relationships and loyalty with their followers. Leading in a global context requires understanding of not just the people but their worldview, customs, local conditions and laws. Developing an *Open Organization* requires leaders to develop humility, inquisitiveness and an earnest desire to build honest connections with those who serve the organization in foreign places. A successful global leader must be more interested in building rapport long before they consider their bottom line. Developing a rapport with their followers, leaders are best able to limit the power distance and to operate within the trust required for all members of an *Open Organization*. Trust requires an interpretation of culture and how we view and interpret the culture is based predominantly on how we see the culture through our own cultural lenses. Cultures are defined by the very filters and lenses by which we base our decisions. Considering the lenses by which we view the world we can begin to consider the worldview of others. It becomes essential for global leaders to adjust their filters and lenses to include other cultural attributes. Because our thoughts are understood to be culturally-based, we begin to view members of a given culture differently and notice that they do not think the same way we do.

The secret formula to leading an *Open Organization* would appear to begin and end with the leader's ability to connect and build trust with those in which they may have to influence. Building trust, while a complex matter, is achievable in most all instances. Trust begins with an understanding of power distances and the defining of the culture as either high- or low-context.

What is clear is that our continuum does not end with Organization 3.0 and open systems. Drivers of change are constantly forcing the evolution of markets and human capital needs. What may emerge in Organization 4.0 and beyond can only be imagined through the use of scenarios and the systematic process of strategic foresight. As we become more aware of our surroundings and the human condition, we are sure to continue seeing leadership and organizational theory evolve beyond our current understanding. Should these trends continue, we are confident in our imagining of a future with many more multicultural, flat, open systems structured leadership and organization styles.

References

Advameg (2011). "Open and Closed Systems" Retrieved on 11/23/2011 from: http://www.referenceforbusiness.com/management/Ob-Or/Open-and-Closed-Systems.html.

Ashkenas, R., Ulrich, D., Jick, T., & Kerr, S. (2002). *The Boundaryless Organization*. Hoboken, NJ: Jossey-Bass.

Bolden, R., Gosling, J., Marturano, A. & Dennison, P (2003). "A review of leadership theory and competency frameworks" *University of Exeter Centre for Leadership Studies*. Exeter, United Kingdom.

Brafman, Ori & Beckstrom, Rod A. (2006). *The Starfish and the Spider*. New York, NY: The Penguin Group.

Branch, Chester (2011). Retrieved from his posting: Blackboard Dialogues for Doctorate in Strategic Leadership, Regent University, Virginia Beach, VA.

Burkus, David (2010). *The Portable Guide to Leading Organizations*. Tulsa. OK: LeaderLab Press.

Caste System. (2013). *In World History: Ancient and Medieval Eras*. Retrieved April 8, 2013, from http://o-ancienthistory2.abc-clio.com.library.regent.edu/

Chaleff, Ira (2003). *The Courageous Follower*. San Francisco, CA: Berrett-Koehler Publishers, Inc.

Clark, D. R. (2004), Instructional System Design Concept Map Retrieved August 24, 2010 from http://www.nwlink.com/~donclark/leader/leadcon.html.

Cornish, Edward (2004). *Futuring. The Exploration of the Future.* Bethesda, MD: World Future Society.

Creswell, John W. (2009). *Research Design, 3rd Edition.* Thousand Oaks, CA: Sage Publications, Inc.

Cummings, T.G. & Worley, C.G. (2001). *Organization Development & Change. 7th Edition.* Mason, OH: South-Western College Publishing.

Daft, Richard L. (2002). *The Leadership Experience. Second Edition.* Mason, OH: South-Western.

Daft, Richard L. (2004). *Organizational Theory and Design.* Mason, OH: South-Western.

Davis, A.L. & Rothstein, H.R. (2006). "The Effects of the Perceived Behavioral Integrity of Managers on Employee Attitudes: A Meta-analysis" *Journal of Business Ethics.* 67:407-419.

de Kluyver, C.A. & Pearce II, J.A. (2009). *Strategy. A view from the Top Third Edition.* Upper Saddle River, NJ: Pearson Prentice Hall.

Docherty, Michael (2006). "Primer on 'open innovation': Principles and practices" *Research Technology Management.* Jul/Aug; 49, 4, p 64.

Eisenberg, E.M. & Goodall Jr., H.L. (2004). *Organizational Communication. Fourth Edition.* Boston, MA: Bedford/St. Martin's.

Elmquist, M., Fredberg, T., & Ollila, S. (2009). "Exploring the field of open innovation" *European Journal of Innovation Management.* Vol. 12 No. 3, p 326-345.

Foster, Philip A. (2011). "*Open Source* as a Leadership and Organizational Model" Presented at the Regent University School of Global Leadership & Entrepreneurship Leading Transformational Innovation Roundtable, May 14 – 15, 2011.

Foster, Philip A. (2011). Retrieved from his posting: Blackboard Dialogues for Doctorate in Strategic Leadership, Regent University, Virginia Beach, VA.

Foster, Philip A. (2011). "The Open Organization: Exploring the implications of Open Systems Theory as an Organizational Model and its impact on the structure, motivation, culture and generational differences of the organizational system." Virginia Beach, Virginia: Regent University LDSL 705, December 4, 2011.

Freeman, R.E., & Stoner, J.A. (1992). *Management 5th Edition*. Englewood Cliffs: Prentice Hall.

Galbraith, Jay R. (2002). *Designing Organizations*. San Francisco, CA: Jossey-Bass.

Gary, Jay (2012). Retrieved from his posting: Blackboard Dialogues for Doctorate in Strategic Leadership, Regent University, Virginia Beach, VA.

Gilbert & Matviuk (2008). "Empirical Research: The Symbiotic Nature of the Leader-Follower relationship and it's impact on Organizational Effectiveness. *Academic Leadership*", Retrieved on March 20, 2013 from http://www.academicleadershiporg/emprical_research/The_Symbiotic_Nature_of_the_Leader-Follower_relationship_and_Its_Impact_on_Organizational_Effectiveness_printer.shtml.

Girod, Christina. (2013). King David. In *World History: Ancient and Medieval Eras*. Retrieved April 8, 2013, from http://0-ancienthistory2.abc-clio.com.library.regent.edu/

Gomes-Casseres, Benjamin (1994). "Groups Versus Group: How Alliance Networks Compete." Retrieved on March 5, 2013 from http://hbr.org/1994/07/group-versus-group-how-alliance-networks-compete.

Gordon, Judith R. (1991). *A Diagnostic Approach to Organizational Behavior. 3rd Edition*. Needham Heights, MA: Allyn and Bacon.

Grace, Douglas (2011). Retrieved from his posting. Blackboard Dialogues for Doctorate in Strategic Leadership, Regent University, Virginia Beach, VA.

Griffin, Dana (n.d.). "Open System Organizational Structure." Retrieved on November 24, 2011 from http://smallbusiness.chron.com/open-system-organizational-structure-432.html.

Hackman, M.Z. & Johnson, C.E. (2000). *Leadership: A Communication Perspective 3rd Edition*. Prospect Heights, IL: Waveland Press, Inc.

Hamel, Gary (2002). *Leading the Revolution*. New York, NY: Penguin Group.

Handy, Charles (1989). *The Age of Unreason*. Boston, MA: Harvard Business School Press.

Hans, J. & Wolfgang K. (2009). *Social Theory: Twenty Introductory Lectures – Translated by Alex Skinner*. New York, NY: Cambridge University Press.

Hesselbein, F. & Goldsmith, M. (2009). *The Organization of the Future*. San Francisco, CA: Jossey-Bass.

Hines, Andy (2006). "Strategic Foresight" *The Futurist*. World Futurist Society. September-October 2006. pp 18 – 21.

Homula, Michael (2010). "Servant Leadership for Real" Retrieved: http://www.bearingfruitconsulting.com/2009/07/servant-leadership-not-so-with-you.html.

Howe, Jeff (2008). *Crowdsourcing. Why the Power of the Crowd is Driving the Future of Business*. New York, NY: Crown Business.

HRMID (2011). "Straight and narrow path to success" *Human Resource Management International Digest*. Vol. 19, No. 2, p 5-7.

Kanter, Rosabeth Moss (1994). "Collaborative Advantage: The Art of Alliances." Retrieved on March 5, 2013 from http://hbr.org/1994/07/collaborative-advantage-the-art-of-alliances/.

Kanungo, R.N. & Mendonca, M. (1996). *Ethical Dimensions of Leadership* Thousand Oaks, CA: Sage Publications, Inc.

Li, Charlene (2010). *Open Leadership* San Francisco, CA: Jossey-Bass.

Marsh, N., McAllum, M., & Purcell, D. (2002). "Why Strategic Foresight?" Retrieved 5/1/2012 from http://www.globalforesight.net/category?Action=View&Category_id=73.

McGuffey, Chris (2012). Retrieved from his posting: Blackboard Dialogues for Doctorate in Strategic Leadership, Regent University, Virginia Beach, VA.

Mendenhall, Mark E. (2011). "Strategic Planning Failure." Retrieved January 25, 2011 from http://www.referenceforbusiness.com/management/Sc-Str/Strategic-Planning-Failure.html.

Mintzberg, H., Ahlstrand, B., & Lampel, J. (1998). *Strategy Safari*. New York, NY: First Free Press.

Morgan, Gareth (2006). *Images of Organization*. Thousand Oaks, CA: Sage Publications, Inc.

Myers, David G. (2007). *Psychology – Eighth Edition*. New York, NY: Worth Publishers.

Nadler, D.A. & Tushman, M.L. (1997). *Competing by Design*. New York, NY: Oxford University Press, Inc.

Northouse, Peter G. (2001). *Leadership Theory and Practice Second Edition*. Thousand Oaks, CA: Sage Publications, Inc.

Open Archives (2011). "Open Architecture" Retrieved on May 2, 2011 from: http://www.openarchives.org/

Open Organizations (2006).The Open Organizations Project. Retrieved May 2, 2001 from: http://www.open-organizations.org/.

O'Mahony, Siobhan (2007). "The governance of Open Source initiatives: what does it mean to be community managed?" *J Manage Governance*. Springer Science+Business Meda, 11:139-150.

O'Toole, James (1996). *Leading Change.* New York, NY: The Random House Publishing Group.

Ousterhout, John (2009). "Open Decision-Making" Retrieved May 2, 2001 from: http://www.stanford.edu/~ouster/cgi-bin/decisions.php .

Penn, Allisen (2008). *Leadership Theory Simplified.* Little Rock, AR: University of Arkansas.

Pitron, John (2008). Followership is Leadership: The Leadership-Exemplary Followership Exchange Model [Internet]. *Version 8. Knol. 2008 Aug 16.* Retrieved from: http://knol.google.com/k/dr-john-pitron/followership-is-leadership/12nb17zejmb1w/2.

Saffo, Paul (2012). "Six Rules for Effective Forecasting." *Harvard Business Review OnPoint.* Summer 2012, pp 72-80.

Schoemaker, Paul, J.H. (2002). *Profiting from Uncertainty.* New York, NY: The Free Press.

Senge, Peter M. (1990). *The Fifth Discipline. The Art and Practice of the Learning Organization.* New York, NY: Doubleday.

Simoes-Brown, David (2009). "Opening up Innovation in the Workplace" *Training Journal.* September, p 50 - 53.

Simons, Tony L. (1999). "Behavioral integrity as a critical ingredient for transformational leadership" *Journal of Organizational Change Management.* Vol. 12, No. 2, p 89-104.

Sire, James W. (1997). *The Universe Next Door.*3rd Edition. Madison, WI: InterVarsity Press.

Smith, Mark K. (1999). 'Learning Theory', *the encyclopedia of informal education.* Retrieved from http://www.infed.org/biblio/b-learn.htm, Last update: September 03, 2009.

Stanford, Naomi (2009). *Guide to Organisation Design.* Pine Street, London: Profile Books, Ltd.

Stanley, Andy (2003). *The Next Generation Leader.* Sisters, OR: Multnomah Publishers, Inc.

Stone, A.G. & Patterson, K. (2005). "The History of Leadership Focus." Servant Leadership Research Roundtable – August 2005, School of Leadership Study, Regent University.

Tamas, Andy (2007). "Geert Hofstede's Dimensions of Culture and Edward T. Hall's Time Orientations." Retrieved on February 17, 2012 from tamas.com.

Vago, Steven (2004). *Social Change. Fifth Edition.* Upper Saddle River, NJ: Pearson Education, Inc.

von Bertalanffy, Ludwig (1968). *General Systems Theory.* Retrieved 11/26/2011 from http://www.panarchy.org/vonbertalanffy/systems.1968.html.

Walton, Mary (1986). *The Deming Management Method.* New York, NY: The Berkley Publishing Group.

Yehuda, Gil (2011). "Becoming an Open Leader" *Gil Yehuda's Enterprise 2.0 Blog.* Retrieved May 2, 2011 from http://www.gilyehuda.com/2011/03/16/open-leadership-book-review/.

Figures

Figure 1: Foster, Philip (2013). "The Timeline of Leadership and Organizational Theory"

About the Author

Dr. Philip A. Foster is a leadership/business coach and consultant and Adjunct Professor. He is a noted Thought Leader in Business Operations, Organizational Development, Foresight and Strategic Leadership. Dr. Foster facilitates change through the design and implementation of strategies, strategic foresight, and planning.

He holds a Masters in Organizational Leadership and a Doctorate of Strategic Leadership. He has published scholarly articles and is the bestselling author of *The Open Organization. A New Era of Leadership and Organizational Development. 2nd Edition.* Maximum Change Press. ISBN: 978-1533320117 and *Organization 3.0 - The Evolution of Leadership and Organizational Theories Toward an Open System for the 21st Century.* Maximum Change Press.

His experience includes over twenty-five years in both public and the private sector including Tier 1 consulting, media, high-tech and public relations.

He can be reached at www.maximumchange.com or on twitter: @maximumchange

Maximum Change, Inc.

The Maximum Change team provides over 60 years of scholarly and applied organizational leadership executive experience. Our senior partners are all Doctor of Strategic Leadership and Foresight candidates who demonstrate performance excellence in both public and private sector organizations.

The advantages to working with Maximum Change:

- Expertise: Highly qualified staff will work to help you achieve your goals.

- Experience: Diverse experience provides well-rounded perspective and insights.

- Flexibility: We customize our approach and solutions to your unique needs

- Teamwork: We partner with you to develop solutions we cannot achieve individually

- Insight: We offer a fresh, unbiased perspective to your organization's challenges and opportunities.

When you hire Maximum Change, you engage a group of professionals with extensive experience in modern leadership practice. We will focus on developing your organization in order to improve performance and successfully manage change. For more information, visit: http://www.maximumchange.com.

Made in the USA
Columbia, SC
20 July 2018